St. Francis and the Wolf of Gubbio

Copyright © 2024 by JSB Morse. All Rights Reserved. Printed in the United States of America.

This book was produced by Libertas Kids, an imprint of Code Publishing, Austin, TX. LibertasKids.com
ISBN 978-1-60020-119-6 Hardcover 978-1-60020-123-3 Ebook ISBN 978-1-60020-120-2

Around 1220 AD, St. Francis lived in the picturesque town of Gubbio, nestled amidst the rolling hills and lush forests of Central Italy. Francis was known for his ardent devotion to God and his compassion for every living creature. Gubbio was a peaceful place, where people and animals lived harmoniously together.

But one day, a fearsome wolf appeared on the outskirts of the town. This wolf was unlike any other; he was aggressive and menacing, and he struck fear into the hearts of all who saw him.

At first, the wolf began by attacking the livestock of the town. But soon, his hunger grew, and he started to prey upon the people of Gubbio. The townsfolk were terrified, for no one knew how to stop the vicious wolf.

The villagers hoped the problem would go away but the situation grew more dire. The wolf became bolder, lurking outside the town gates and attacking anyone who dared to venture beyond. The people of Gubbio lived in fear, and they pleaded with their leaders to find a solution.

Francis, hearing of the plight of the town, knew he had to do something to help. "What do you have to fear?" he asked them. "Nothing. Whom do you have to fear? No one. Why? Because whoever has joined forces with God obtains three great privileges: omnipotence without power, intoxication without wine, and life without death. We must remember from Holy Scripture that 'perfect love cast out all fear.'"

But the villagers all grumbled at Francis's words. The women of the village blamed the men for not standing up to the threat and the men all blamed each other for not having the courage to face the terrifying beast.

Finally, despite the scoffs and warnings of the villagers, Francis volunteered to confront the ferocious animal himself with nothing but a cross for protection.

With a small group of followers by his side, Francis ventured beyond the safety of the town walls and into the wilderness where the wolf was said to dwell.

As they approached the wolf's lair, they could hear the beast's menacing growls growing louder and louder. The wolf beheld the group of humans and it charged toward Francis with its snarling jaws.

Francis traced the sign of the cross and shouted, "I command you to cease your reign of terror in the name of God!" Miraculously, the wolf slowed down and trotted calmly to him and rested at his feet, gently placing its head in Francis's hands.

With authority and compassion, Francis spoke: "Brother wolf, you have done much evil in this land, destroying and killing the creatures of God without his permission. Not only animals have you killed but you have even dared to devour men, made in the image of God! For that, you're worthy of being hanged like a robber and a murderer. All men cry out against you, the dogs pursue thee, and all the inhabitants of this city are thy enemies; but I will make peace between you and them, O brother wolf. If you will stop offending them, they shall forgive you all your past offenses, and neither men nor dogs shall pursue you any more."

The wolf showed its agreement with a bow and a nod and Francis stood up and commanded the wolf to follow him into town.

Arriving at the bustling piazza, a crowd had gathered to witness the miraculous event. With the wolf by his side Francis declared, "My fellow citizens of Gubbio, you have let your fear of this beast drive you to hate. But how much we rather ought to dread the jaws of Hell, if the jaws of so small an animal as a wolf can make a whole city tremble through fear?"

"Friends, where there is love and wisdom, there is neither fear nor ignorance. Where there is worship of God, there no enemy can enter. Therefore, I present to you not an enemy, but a companion and a friend. And if you will provide nourishment for God's creation, he will never again cause pain to this village." Then, on behalf of the wolf, Francis offered the people peace. In a resounding chorus, the villagers applauded and cheered.

Turning to the wolf, Francis asked if it would live in peace under these terms. With a humble bow of its head and a graceful twist of its body, the wolf conveyed its acceptance placing its paw in Francis's hand, sealing the pact.

From that day onward, the people of Gubbio honored their promise. The wolf lived peacefully among them for two years, going from door to door for sustenance. It harmed no one, and no one harmed it. Even the dogs ceased to bark in its presence.

When the wolf passed away from old age, the people mourned. Its peaceful presence had reminded them of the virtues and holiness of St. Francis, and of the providence of the living God.

During renovations of Saint Francis of Peace church in Gubbio in 1872, the centuries-old skeleton of a large wolf was discovered outside near the foundations. The people of Gubbio chose to give these remains a burial inside the church. As St. Francis wished, Brother Wolf of Gubbio rests in peace.

The End

For more great children's books visit LibertasKids.com

www.ingramcontent.com/pod-product-compliance
Lightning Source LLC
Chambersburg PA
CBHW041603070526
44586CB00003BA/63